BLUE INK TEARS

Blue Ink Tears: A Collection of Poems
Roberto Germán

ISBN: 979-8-9872072-1-5

Editor: Tanya Manning-Yarde
Spanish Translation: Jasmín García Ramírez
Cover and Text Designs: Monica Ann Cohen
Photography: Fresh Creativo

www.multiculturalclassroom.com
Instagram, Facebook, LinkedIn, TikTok: Multicultural Classroom
Twitter: @RGerman2012

DEDICATION

To my children, Analíz, Zion and Sol:
from my heart to yours.

12/10/09

(1)

PART 3
Every Day Livi[ng]
1. Found Her
2. Stay Alive
7. Baseball &
12. Nothing Lik[e]

PART 2
Relationshi[p]
1. Sweri[n]g
5 Carame[l]
8 Still
11. Angel[ic]

PART 1
Race +
1. Still, A[merican]

Relationships

Divorce   Final Moments
Still Night   Mom's Stress
Caramel   Found Her
Our Faith   Past Tense
Swerving   Blue Ink Tears

Identity

Still, American
Café con Le[che]
Black Deni[al]
Spanish
Truthful Ro[ots]

Portraits/Scenes

Baseball
His Faith
Angelic
   Tia Reb
   Stay Alive
Ru[s]ell
Ye
Marching Man
   My Ghetto

[...n/Ford]

BLUE

1. Angelic
2. Tia Rebecca
3. Our Faith
4. A Mother's Struggle
5. Purple Flower
6. Petals
7. Past Tense
8. Still Night / Night, Still
9. Caramel
10. Swerving
11. Blue Ink ~~Tears~~

INK

1. Marching Man
2. My People
3. My Ghetto
4. City of Promise
5. Unexpected Tension
6. Café Con Leche
7. Lengua
8. Spanish
9. Truthful Roots
10. Black Denial
11. Still, American
12. A Mission

Pancakes 6. Lizards Frogs TE...
Moments 5. Sweet Dreams
Russell "Shoes" Rejection
ce it His Faith 15. Mosquito

le
with 3 A Mother's Struggle
8 Flower 7 Past Tense BLUE
Blue Ink Tears Flat Pets
etals

Relationship
Portrait
Angelic ⟩ Mom/son
        love
Shoes ⟩ race struggle/longing
   Tia Rebeca ⟩ family faith womanhood
                                  Portrait
A Moth's Struggle ⟩ mother family relations
                    class
Faith ⟩ faith portrait immigration
         MLK politics activism
                              ...ness ...uito ⟩ earth

Spanish ⟩ haiku language
              colonization
Purple Flower ⟩ earth
Café con leche ⟩ food ic...
                   Domi...
Lengua ⟩ languag...
Blue Ink Tears ⟩ love rel...
Past Tense ⟩ love, relati...
Swerving ⟩ love r...
Still Night ⟩ love
Found Her ⟩ bask...
             perso...
Caramel ⟩ f...
Nothing Like ⟩ lif...
the First ⟩ boy h...
Final Moment...
Unexpected ...
Rejection ⟩ ide...

Lizards Frogs ⟩ earth humor

TEARS
1. Syrup & Pancakes
2. Lizards
3. Mosquito
4. Stay Alive
5. Sweet Dreams
6. Shoes
7. Found Her
8. Baseball
9. They Call Him Corny
10. Pride
11. Divorce
12. Rejection
13. Noth...

...le ⟩ caution
    portrait hot take
             Russell Wilson ⟩ character
                              portrait

...h
...nification
...ymbol

CONTENTS

BLUE   1

Angelic   *2*

Tía Rebecca   *4*

Tía Rebecca   *5*

Truly, Truly, I Say to You   *8*

En Verdad, En Verdad, Les Digo   *9*

A Mother's Struggle   *10*

Purple Flower   *12*

Petals   *13*

Sunrise, Sunset   *16*

Still Night/Night, Still   *17*

Past Tense   *18*

Caramel   *19*

Swerving   *20*

Blue Ink Tears   *21*

INK   23

Marching Man   *24*

My People   *26*

My Ghetto   *27*

City of Promise   *28*

Unexpected Tension   *30*

Café Con Leche   *33*

Lengua   *34*

Spanish   *36*

Español   *37*

Black Denial   *38*

Yo Soy Un Plátano   *39*

Truthful Roots   *40*

Raíces Veraces   *41*

Mapping My Blackness   *42*

In the Motherland   *43*

A Mission   *44*

TEARS   47

Syrup & Pancakes   *48*
Lizards   *49*
Mosquito   *50*
Mosquito   *51*
Stay Alive   *52*
Sweet Dreams   *53*
Shoes   *54*
Zapatos   *55*
Found Her   *56*
They Call Him Corny   *58*
Baseball   *60*
Anger   *62*
Pride   *66*
Divorce   *67*
Radio Silence   *68*
Stress   *69*
Rejection   *70*
Nothing Like The First   *72*
His Faith   *74*
Su Fe   *75*
Final Moments   *78*
Momentos Finales   *79*

GLOSSARY   82

ACKNOWLEDGMENTS   84

BLUE

Angelic

Joy of your heart
nestled in your womb
hum me tunes
it's not too soon

Your angelic voice
helps me feel soothed
bond so tender
between me and you

Caress me softly
this life you now hold
release the 10 months
a moment quite bold

Wrap me in terrycloth
abound in grace
lil' ole me
a new space awaits

Carry me gently
sway as you move
pressed on your chest
just me and you

Rock me to sleep
rhythm of comfort
your melody
peace to my slumber

Listen to me breathe
as I listen to your heart beat
a beautiful sound
we both fall asleep

Care for me
things only you notice
attention to details
deep focus

Kisses and hugs
bring plenty of warmth
warmth that only
you can put forth

Tía Rebecca

The only aunt my mother truly knew
after school she welcomed her with home-made bread
I make bread now, too
lineage and history through my hands

I remember the way my father wheeled her in the grass
past the parishioners
no one stopped her
from attending the church picnic

Rebecca Hilton Johnson had mustard-seed faith
when rest was far away
her resistance amidst the storm
increased all the more
as if allergic to adversity

Difficult times
didn't translate to
dismissed devotion
praise turned up

Counted it all joy
complaints tucked away
like in a cupboard
reserved for only her

A godly woman
whose sacred faith
expressed a positive attitude
towards the future
unwavering trust in the Lord

A prayer warrior
when presented with your problems
would take them to the Upper Room
and come out victorious

Tía Rebecca

La única tía que mi madre realmente conoció
después de la escuela la recibió con pan casero
Yo también hago pan ahora
linaje e historia a través de mis manos

Recuerdo la forma en que mi padre la rodaba en su silla de
ruedas por la hierba
más allá de los feligreses
nadie la detuvo
de asistir al pícnic de la iglesia

Rebecca Hilton Johnson tenía una fe de semilla de mostaza
cuando el descanso estaba lejos
su resistencia en medio de la tormenta
aumentó aún más
como si fuera alérgica a la adversidad

Tiempos difíciles
no causaron una
devoción despedida
elevaron alabanzas
Todo lo contó como alegría
quejas escondidas
como en un armario
reservado solo para ella

Una mujer piadosa
cuya sagrada fe
expresó una actitud positiva
hacia el futuro
confianza inquebrantable en el Señor

Una guerrera de oración
cuando se le presentaron tus problemas
los llevaba al Aposento Alto
y salía victoriosa

Rebeca Hilton Johnson

Nacio el 20 de Junio, 1916
Samana, Republica Dominicana

Sus Hijos; Ana Luisa Angenor,
Jorge Ray, Ana Maria Reding,
Rafael Hilton, Antonio Shepard,
Cesar Hilton, Otilia Medina,
Ruben Hilton, Gloria Diaz.
Sus Nietos, Bi-Nietos, Hermanos,
Sobrinos, y demas Familiares,
Pasamos por el profundo dolor
de perder a nuestra Madre...

Gracias Mama por darnos
85 años de inmenso Amor.

He Peleado la buena batalla,
He acabado la carerra,
He guardado la fe,
Por lo demas, me esta guardada
la corona de Justicia, la cual
me dara el Señor Jesus,
Juez Justo en aquel dia.
- 2 Timoteo 4:7

Truly, Truly, I Say to You

Our faith has to be
bigger than our trust in others;
they will disappoint

En Verdad, En Verdad Les Digo

Nuestra fe tiene que ser
más grande que nuestra confianza en los demás;
ellos decepcionarán

A Mother's Struggle

Disregarded by children
whose disrespect had the stench of spoiled milk
manipulated
cast guilt
wasted her money
again and again
Sweated and sewed
worked overtime
black dye tried to hide
the gray strands that ran down her shoulders
she looked older than her age
in need of rest

Like a trip around the sun
her birthday came and went
they dropped by saying "I can't stay long"
she was an afterthought

The world couldn't stop her
from being a giving tree
of warm meals
bills paid
advice given
late rides
doctors visits
problems solved...

Arms open wide like a General Sherman
stretched beyond capacity
receiving her children's burdens
in truth and in lies

A steadfast commitment
to guide them along the right path
the narrow road she envisioned for them
became lonely
when they ultimately strayed

Backtalk felt like a backhand
tested patience
ignored tears
high blood pressure
swollen eyes
her cries landed on deaf ears

She died with a pensive smile on her face
taking with her the thought
that one day
they might understand
a mother's struggle, too
crossed arms and nothing left to give
she bid them adieu

Purple Flower

Lovely
this lavender that can be
used to adorn
used to soothe
used to rub

Don't forget to water it

Petals

Petals fall off of a flower
heavy rain drops leave bruises
reminds me
not everything good lasts forever
things can fall apart
a humble unraveling
sorrow
freshness fades from today to tomorrow

Petals fall off of a flower
and remind me
not everything good lasts forever
they dampen like t-shirts wet with tears
from a breakup
torn to pieces
hopeful to make amends
scraps of her heart roam in search of the love we once had

Blue Ink Tears

A Celebration of Young Art & Culture In The Merrimack Valley

Join us for a FREE evening of poetry, music and dance!

**Rogers Center for the Arts
Merrimack College
North Andover, MA**

With guest appearances by nationally renowned performers!

**Friday, October 25
7:00 - 9:00pm**

Come see the future of arts in our area.
Local artisans will display their works and some will be available for purchase.

Refreshments will be available

BSU is a multicultural organization that celebrates and promotes all cultures in Merrimack College and other communities. Our vision is to provide a community support for all who wish to participate and to educate its members and the college community about the diverse student body.

Blue Ink Tears: *Friday, October 25th, 2002 (7-9pm)*

(*Brief*) Introduction by Roberto German and Jackson Garcia

I. Shantell Cuevas singing "Fallin'" by Alicia Keys featuring Carlos Rodriguez

II. Hope Street Spoken Word

III. Hope Street Dance #1

IV. Troy Lazaro from The Soul Kaliber Movement

V. KAYLA

VI. Kailin Diaz

VII. Lawrence Ballet Academy

VIII. Carlos Rodriguez singing "Waters Run Dry" by Boyz II Men featuring Juan Lopez

IX. Anthony Morales

X. Intermission

XI. Talia Lazaro and Sheena Hatchett

XII. V2

XIII. Spyder Crew

XIV. Lamar McLaughlin from The Soul Kaliber Movement

XV. Rosalee

XVI. Roberto German from The Soul Kaliber Movement featuring KAYLA, Melissa Metivier, and Melquis Rodriguez

XVII. Hope Street Drama #2

XVIII. Jackson Garcia from The Soul Kaliber Movement

XIX. Jonathan Cabrera from The Soul Kaliber Movement

XX. Hope Street Dance #2

(*Brief*) Conclusion Roberto German and Jackson Garcia

Sunrise, Sunset

We watch the sun rise
side by side we sit in awe
beauty beholds us

Top of the morning
simplicity of sunup
nature takes its course

Seizing the moment
together we chase the sun
as we exchange smiles

Like radiant beams
hope sits on the horizon
and it feels pleasant

To hold hands and stroll
'round the reservoir again
before it gets dark

With so much to say
the two of us converse 'til
the day is complete

Longing to stay but
sundown signals the little
time that we have left

We watch the sun set
side by side we sit in awe
my first date with you

Still Night/Night, Still

Head on hand
pad on pause
eyes on mind
mind on thoughts

Memory on love
love on hold
hold on you

You don't know
know this love
come in close
for this hug

Why do we
play these games?
say we won't
go and play
please don't go
you can stay
say we won't
then still play

Up all night
like it's still
stuck in time
let's be real
still it's night
we're still up
looking like
"Baby, what's up?"

Past Tense

An ear-to-ear grin as the wheels turn in my mind
Kodak moments cycle through
these pictures are far from perfect

Good times with our fingers intertwined
on the white roller coaster at Canobie Lake Park
the mutual vibes
remember that?

Friendly flirtation amongst adolescents

In the back of the church van we whispered and cuddled
the others were jealous of our chemistry
as if they were in a class which they did not ask to be enrolled in

But teenage love tends to not care what other people think
it studies itself while wearing blinders
bite-size expressions on Post-it notes that document all the feels
nor journal pages nor adults can contain the so-called drama
and we were all caught up in it
weren't we?

The Youth Pastor pleaded and pestered
for us to leave room for the Holy Ghost
even though we all knew
that our faithful attendance
was more about being present
with each other
wasn't it?

I'm trippin'
that was then
then again, I can barely recall it
short-lived, but cute while it lasted

A thing of the past
right?

Caramel

A premium sauce
runs from the top
with an ooze
smooth
head to toe
there's a glow
want her to know
she's my
caramel
my preferred flavor
when I'm salty
irritable
she's still sweet
irresistible
mi dulce de leche
fills me
with her goodness
a slow melt
wrapped in her warmth
buttery smell
savory and rich
the perfect complement
to this dish

Swerving

171 mile drive
2 hr 34 min
in the middle of the night
to see you
tolls on the fastest route
fiending
quick glances at the speed limit
shift in gears
switch from slow to fast lane
a challenge: take our phone conversation
face to face
see you smirk again
vibe with you
swerve with sarcasm
no gas stop
one more exit closer to you
a look in the rearview
no flashing lights
adrenaline rush
past the stop sign
reach in the glove compartment
grab the cologne
two sprays of CK One
one hand on the wheel
thoughts of you in my arms
even if for one night

Blue Ink Tears

Nervous glances caught your attention

Now memory speed dials your name and number
an unforgettable connection

My tender spot
the object of my affection
cupid's arrow
I'm into you
you're into me
still, no you and me?

I pursue we
but you don't pursue me?
I over pursue the possibility
but you're not committed
I'm confused…
my vision is blurred
tears dissolve my romance
and I wish I never met her
heart and mind misaligned
I allowed my heart to feel
thought I was immune to being lovesick

Romantic revelations
determine the way my pen moves
distress, anguish and pain
swollen eyes and a torn spirit
paper crumpled and ripped
a faux smile can't masquerade
the mood on my face

I shut down and pull away
talk to myself
until I no longer listen
blue ink tears write
on this page

INK

Marching Man

A poem for M.L.K., Jr.

Marching Man
from Selma to sorrow
Mobile to madness
Birmingham to blues

Marching Man
from Atlanta to altercations
Savannah to sadness
Tucker to tribulations

Marching Man
through landmines for liberation
barriers broken
in the deep South

Marching Man
seeking God's kingdom
tested and tempered
unashamed and unapologetic

Marching Man
narrator of knowledge
pursuer of progress
example of excellence

Marching Man
sacrificial father
blessed husband
son, brother, friend

Marching Man
leader of a movement
center of controversy
principled and persuasive

Marching Man
from Selma to sorrow
Mobile to madness
Birmingham to blues

Marching Man
Lawrence to Austin to Tampa
organize, reconcile, and build
me, you, us

Marching Man
your words
your passion
live through me

Marching Man
the journey's long
but you showed how
to be strong

We march now
hope our march
will make you proud
Marching Men

My People

My people, separate but equal,
still must demand equity
no longer do we have segregated facilities
instead separated by perceived abilities

Are we so naïve as to believe
where systems of oppression exist, people are actually free?
where we are killed while saying "I can't breathe"?
our history books don't say a peep about Indigenous sweeps
while we sit on land that ain't ours to keep
a country built off the soul of Black folks whose souls still weep

There's praise for those of us that whitewash our ways
abandon culture, change names
to desperately assimilate

We're supposed to be United but can't even get voters' rights right
left, right, left
blue, red
red, blue
it's bruised purple

Body hurts from the fight
bean bags blasted
chants of "No justice, no peace"
threats of take over
imposed neighbors bring their Starbucks
imposed school leaders turn us around until we're dizzy
imposed authority
we didn't create the policies that govern this society
we're just part of the irony

My Ghetto

Where houses stand for nothing
and nothing stands for humanity
humanity stands for struggle
struggle stands for existence
existence stands for immigration
immigration stands for separation
separation stands for nostalgia
nostalgia stands for longing
longing stands for longsuffering

City of Promise

I'm from the City of LAWRENCE
birthplace of poets, Roberto & Robert
frosted in proverbs
to quote Solomon, "The mouth of a fool brings ruin near"
so, here's to Jay Atkinson
who babbled about that which he did not know, does not know
and will not know

Cause some things have to be experienced to be understood
big ups, to What's Good in the Hood!
real journalists portray the truth with authenticity
reporting live from the intersection of Esperanza & Hope St.
my folks be leading movements in this City of Promise
the great City of Lawrence where it's common to hear people
say,
I never knew a luh, luh, luh, a love like this
Gotta be somethin' for me to write this

See, I am a voice in the wilderness, too
my city is not screwed
media bias in news
but history's coming alive through the youth
Briyith Betances, Mass Youth of the Year
we breed the best & brightest round here

It's a habit in this Habitat for Humanity
where we hold hands
work together to balance the scales of depravity
meet me at the center of gravity

Like a blind date... there's ALWAYS HOPE that this will turn
out well
and since damned is related to hell, there's NO WAY in hell MY
CITY is damned!

my city is jam-packed with immigrants who left everything in
order to give everything
a recurring history in these streets where residents pursue
happiness like Will Smith

Against all odds
relentlessly working to overcome the obstacles: language,
culture, customs and
systems of oppression
an ongoing mission that's constantly evolving
the spirit of the city captured in a collective voice that cries out,
WE ARE LAWRENCE
The CITY of PROMISE

Unexpected Tension

Black fist metal pick nestled in thick hair
big hair don't care that's what I'm gon' wear
wear my emotions on my sleeve
that's what my White mentor told me

When I told him I'm leaving
the school we both loved
because the ceiling was low
whenever I looked up
no chance to grow
it was time to go
wondered if it had anything to do with how I glowed

This was fairly common at a PWI
hard to see the underrepresented truly climb
many reservations
tried to tell him why
but his lens was too blurred to see it through my eyes

Unexpected tension took a toll
thought it was a joke . . .
'til he he hung up the phone
this is what happened to me when I wouldn't fold
when I wouldn't shut my mouth
do as I was told

Chose to venture out
try to do it on my own
but he refused to see me as mature, fully grown
determined to move forward
vacated my role
my mentor and former teachers went from friends to foes

Got an offer from a rival school
they said I shouldn't go
they said that it was lily White
as if I didn't know
independent thinker I was not to be controlled
control was something other people thought they could hold
over me, citing prior opportunities
like the tuition-assistance I received during my teens

Remaining balance, an invisible debt
I'd be lying if I said it didn't hurt, I wept
"He's disloyal and selfish.
Look at how he paid us back after we helped him."

My thank you was no longer welcome
Went from poster boy to the lost son
mud on my name, attempts to defame my character
rumors 'bout Roberto, they tried to change the narrative
You could hear the disbelief in my laughter
Began to view my mentor and former teachers as actors

High praise, often viewed as saviors
someone save 'em from their own behavior
the complex became more complex
it's industrial, I saw through the nonsense

The strings attached to gifts from philanthropists
the good old boys' network, the chess moves, the politics
I was told I was a Benedict
when my service was no longer for their benefit

They were applauded and awarded
celebrated syndrome where power gets hoarded
imperial ways like colonial days
tried to keep what I made but they were still at the gate

Looked him dead in his eyes, said every word to his face
"Thought that you of all people would offer an embrace."
onto bigger and better, kept it moving with grace
his reaction, quite the opposite
to my distaste

Felt deep pain when we broke our ties
sudden shift in energy
no good vibes
I was excommunicated
no goodbye
saw him in public
he wouldn't shake my hand
no lie
but I started from the bottom
I was destined to rise with my

Black fist metal pick nestled in thick hair
big hair don't care that's what I'm gon' wear
wear my emotions on my sleeve
I only know how to be me

Café Con Leche

Ah! The taste of café con leche
blend of coffee and milk

Island fresh beans imported to The States
mixed to form one from two

Old traditions held firm
introduced to customs anew

Azúcar
melts into the coffee and milk

A compromise
a sweet flavor

The deliciousness of both sides
but

The café cannot assimilate to the point of only being leche
it loses its essence

¡Sabor!
bebiendo despacio

Heritage in each drink
de café con leche

*Café Con Leche was first published in the book *Ni De Aquí, Ni De Alla*

Lengua

Mi batalla con el lenguaje
is nothing short of complicado
soy un poquito de todo
pero completamente nada

Dominican made
American raised
a remix of Spanish and inglés
the pulse of la tambora and upright organ

My words are inglés sin barreras
but my español is not exactly un poema
I forget the femenino
it's always un problema

I lean on my instincts
sometimes confused
I look for the right punctuation
Tía Susana says search down yonder

That's the English of Samaná

I'm tired from the mental struggle
constant doubt
one way in my mind, another out my mouth

Saboreando limoncillos in Haina or
eating pb&j with my boys
when we talk
it's a serving of avocados and concón

Sancocho's heartiness on my lengua
mix of meat and roots
a stew that feeds my español
the sazón makes my adjectives tasty

Cause that's my tongue
mi estilo de hablar
a veces refleja la calle
but it always represents my heart

Lengua was first published in the book *Ni De Aquí, Ni De Alla*

Spanish

Sounds romantic but
colonization did not
practice chivalry

Español

Suena romántico pero
la colonización no
practica la cortesía

Black Denial

I am a part of that
digging for the artifacts
well, here are the facts

Black denial
hair straightening products for your peinao
colonial derizao

"Oye primo
when did you accept the idea that
your piel
wasn't sweet like miel?"

Entangled in bleached beliefs
self hate so deep
through skin it seeps

The African roots play la tambora
rhythm of colorismo on Trujillo's hora
Spanish secrets stored in our historia

Interesante a quien menospreciamos
y a quien glorificamos
a quien, con nuestras estatuas, honramos

Las aguas corren ondo
and claims of not being Black persist
instead: indio   trigueño   moreno
branded with labels I stand

Yo Soy Un Plátano

Yo soy un plátano
Verde y fuerte
I stand tall and proudly represent mi gente
My skin is thick
For sure, seguro
And I'm stronger than other crops
Because soy el maduro
Ripe for the picking
Cuatro por peso sounds nice with some chicken
Hmm, hmm, hmm, hmm . . . finger-licking good!

Truthful Roots

The young man   knee-deep
in black dirt   his hands

Search and   sift
touching   limestone

Blocked   from going further
rocked   to the core

Desperately   in need of tools
to drill   hammer   wedge

Between   the seams
creating   cracks

Attempts to   unearth
buried   truths

Redirected roots   run rampant
He seeks   their origins

On home   soil
and lesser   known terrain

Nowhere near   done digging
the pickaxe   thrashes the ground

Like his head   into his hands
face covered   in dirt

Too many   unanswered questions
deep sigh   as if to say

This is   simply the start
and I   already feel

Crushed   to nothingness

Raíces Veraces

El joven
en tierra negra

hasta las rodillas
sus manos

Busca y
tocando

tamiza
piedra caliza

Bloqueado
sacudido

de ir más lejos
hasta la médula

Desesperadamente
para perforar

necesitando herramientas
martillar   acuñar

Entre
creando

las juntas
grietas

Intentos por
verdades

desenterrar
sepultadas

Raíces redirigidas
Él busca

que corren desenfrenadas
sus orígenes

en suelo
y terreno

natal
menos conocido

Nada cerca
el pico

de terminar de excavar
golpea el suelo

Como su cabeza
cara cubierta

entre las manos
de tierra

Demasiadas
profundo suspiro

preguntas sin respuesta
como diciendo

Esto es
y ya

simplemente el comienzo
me siento

Aplastado

a la nada

Mapping My Blackness

Born in the United States
I am Black
father's from Haina
Black as charcoal
mother's from Samaná
a port town
formerly enslaved Americans escaped to freedom there
Old English catch phrases like go round yonder

Somewhere between
West Africa
Dominican Republic
and Lawrence
exists me
the man in the middle of the Middle Passage

I am Black, beautiful and bold
Dominicans, no need to roam
in our Blackness we are home

In the Motherland

On African soil
diasporic son returns
still, American

A Mission

Daily I dream of
a time when all people groups
will live peacefully

TEARS

Syrup & Pancakes

Smell of maple syrup
taste of pancakes
drool runs down my mouth

A cool and warm combo
I desire to devour this deliciousness
to have it settle in me

The slow brown drip
rolls off the golden crust
knife and fork cut triangles

My teeth dig in
my tongue tastes the slab of butter
slapped on top

I'm a flapjack fanatic fiending for the flavor
savoring
every
sugary
bite
until it's all gone

Lizards

Sun-bathing lizards
live their best lives in Tampa
dwell in homes rent-free

Mosquito

You circled me
dizzying
snuck into the mosquito net
eager to strike
like a phlebotomy intern
menacing, buzzing in my ear
with nothing to say
grazed my skin
torturous tactic
invasion of space
bloodsucker!
Seethed to slap you senseless
you satisfy your hunger
with my meaty hand
you got me,
again!
Swollen
agitated
itchy
short nails
unable to scratch
foolishly lost my cool
chased you
paused
came to my senses
waited patiently
until you got tired
down from your high
my palm facing your eyes
was the last thing you saw

Mosquito

Me rodeaste
mareándome
te colaste en el mosquitero
ansioso por atacar
como un interno en flebotomía
amenazante, zumbando en mi oído
sin nada que decir
rozaste mi piel
táctica torturante
invasión del espacio
¡chupasangre!
Hervía por abofetearte sin sentido
satisfaces tu hambre
con mi mano carnosa
me tienes,
¡otra vez!
Hinchado
agitado
picas
uñas cortas
incapaz de rascarme
tontamente perdí la calma
te perseguí
en pausa
volví a mis sentidos
esperé pacientemente
hasta que te cansaste
bajaste de tu altura
mi palma frente a tus ojos
fue lo último que viste

Stay Alive

Black men like me
are just trying to
jog two miles into the Shores
sit in our living room and eat ice cream
retreat at Twin Lakes while visiting relatives
just
trying
to
stay
alive

Sweet Dreams

I need a break like Kit Kat
wish I could escape to Milky Way
get away from these riff-raff Sour-Patch Kids
rain passes as I sit back and wait to taste the rainbow
but I see no Skittles in the sky, not even a Starburst

Still, I Chuckle and wonder...
what if the plot twisted like Twizzlers?
if my life wasn't so Nutrageous?
feel all wrapped up like a Tootsie Roll
wish I had a Life Saver

Since I need a break and try to get away, I get a Snickers
then, it melts all over my Butterfingers and life only gets worse!
it's like I am a Nerd and I've lost all my Jelly Beans
it's hard to be a Jolly Rancher when you feel like an Airhead
I need a break like Kit Kat.

Shoes

They stay on the shelf a long time
far longer than the others
black on black, smooth leather, crispy clean, thick soles
the others are supposedly a better fit
even if they're a size too small or too big

Undervalued
underutilized
despite their all-purpose capabilities
perfect candidates to win the race
sprint or marathon
dependable
trustworthy

Judged by their color
perceived to cause discomfort
purchasers don't understand their worth
not seen as mainstream
viewed as a disruptor

No opportunity to run the race
no exposure to the world
like knotted laces
all tied up

Zapatos

Se quedan en el estante mucho tiempo
mucho más tiempo que los demás
negro sobre negro, cuero liso, limpio crujiente, suelas gruesas
los otros supuestamente se ajustan mejor
incluso si son de un tamaño más pequeño o más grande

Devaluado
infrautilizado
a pesar de su capacidad multipropósito
candidatos perfectos para ganar la carrera
corta o maratón
dependiente
confiable

Juzgados por su color
percibido por causar incomodidad
los compradores no entienden su valor
no se ven como corriente principal
vistos como interruptor

Sin oportunidad de correr la carrera
sin exposición al mundo
como cordones anudados
completamente atados

Found Her

Found her on the park bench all alone
it was getting dark then
asked if I could walk her home
ever since that walk we been, we been, we been
together, together, together

Always drawn to her
when she was away I would long for her
they told me to pass but, no sir
hit the pavement with a hard bounce as I observed

On time, on target
made a hesitation move but she stuck with me regardless
been with others that were heartless
yet she never crossed over even when courted the hardest

How many times did she forgive me for the bricks?
'til I got her in heavy rotation, swish
sounds beautiful, poetry in motion
like a finger roll, suitable

To get around the defense, they pressured me
returned the favor with a flagrant, happily
called a timeout to figure out the strategy
executed the play masterfully

Even when they sent the whole squad after me
took a charge, did it ever so naturally
always kept it real
caught opponents with 'bows to their grills

Full pivot to create space
we chose to drive the lane at the right pace
Euro-step to avoid the mess, crafty
the things I did to keep her happy

The love never stopped
overtime for her, no game clock
knew that was my last shot
had to take my best shot

Found her on the park bench all alone
it was getting dark then
asked if I could walk her home
ever since that walk we been, we been, we been
together, together, together

They Call Him Corny

For Russell Wilson

Haters love to shade
a good optimistic dude
wretchedness preferred

guas Corren ondo

tent claims of not bein

e used to support the arg

specious

a social construction tha

~~xities of identity format~~

~~of self-identification and~~

ing

16th Century Concept cr

umenbach

ings people together, race

that we experience the

entity formation

Baseball

I
Though I've been hard at work
I'm in a slump like bad posture
this has been a tough stretch
feel tight, need to get loose
I move towards the batter's box
where rocks get pitched

II
Get on base echoes high-pitched
bases loaded and I need to get this work
time to think out the box
forward head posture
A few swings to get loose
full body extension and stretch

III
The pitcher winds up to deliver the speedball as far as his arm
can stretch
don't chase the white rock that's over pitched
the small voice offers its 2 cents like change that is loose
I hold the thought but decide not to put that counsel to work
with a bend and tilt I make contact and alleviate my posture
finally, a hit and I abandon the box

IV
Now my mind plays tricks like a full box
as I run up the 1st base line and kick dust, my hamstrings fully
stretch
adrenaline rushes me to 2nd where I plant myself as if a tent
was pitched
stride, direction and posture
this might be some of my best work
or so I think as I advance to 3rd on the loose

V
The ends are loose
in an attempt to steal home plate, the origins of the box
I underestimate the work
misjudge the final stretch
like a whiff when the ball curves after it's pitched
it stifles me and stiffens my posture

VI
Sick to my stomach I double over in a stooped posture
screws and bowels both loose
the inflated confidence escapes, with it a scream high-pitched
muscles twitch, paranoia makes me want to hide in a box
I dust myself off from the ground as I stretch
and attempt to get back to work

VII
I know my posture might last be viewed in a box
for the loose, death seems like a stretch
the pitched-battle continues as the reliever slings me that work

Anger

Starts as
a simmer
ever so
slightly ignited
sparked light

Low lit
released heat
produces smoke
enough for
anyone around
to get
choked up

A fire
that burns
and consumes
all that
stands in
its way

One assumes
that it
can always
be contained
but the
fumes of
fury from
hidden irritation
are fierce

Red hot
sudden rage
spreads fast
hisses, crackles
feels explosive

A combustion
that has
the potential
to disrupt
any sense
of trust

When words
of wrath
are like
fuel from
the mouth
it's a
chemical reaction
there's nothing
good that
can happen

Even after
it's extinguished
you can
see, smell
and feel
the damage
that will
need to
be restored

Pride

For Ye

Sway did have the answer
you simply would not listen;
a haughty spirit

Divorce

Every other week
fifty percent custody
bags packed, heart broken

Radio Silence

Muting the volume
is at times necessary
to hear one's own voice

Stress

The gut growls
and gas gets going
like a leak
cramps creep
inside intestines
seemingly signs of strain
set spasms in motion

Some say
mind over matter
but my mind's on the latter

Live, love, laugh
sounds so simple
wish it was
but this fart's finna
rip the rug

Rejection

I don't deal well with rejection
it weighs down my mind
makes my body tense
can feel it in my chest
like 3 sets of 10 reps
270 lbs on the flat bench

Stressed to the max
vexed and out of balance
got axed on something
I thought was a lock
makes me feel like a dumbbell

Results of an ego on steroids
head swollen
until reality checks in
and sucks the air out

Left on the decline
bar above head
felt within reach
then weakness increased
to lift that thought
from my brain to this page
was a strenuous task

I don't deal well with rejection
couple of deadlifts and I'm dead
somebody lift me up
like a military press
need a pick me up

Perhaps a protein shake
with some boost?
uh, it's no use
enthusiasm is curbed
excitement is too

Where's my motivation
to pull myself up
and get my chin
above the bar
while I hold a tight
grip on reality?

Nothing Like the First

Nothing like the first day of middle school
first time walking to school alone
first time being late
first time skipping school with your boys
first detention

First crush
first written poems
first kiss
first love letter
first love

First haircut independent of your father
first pair of Nikes
first sunglasses
first jersey
first fitted hat

First honor roll
first yearbook signatures
first banquet
first voted most likely to succeed
first graduation

First year of high school
first pimple
first chest hairs
first time making out
first time calling a girl by another girl's name

First basket scored
first home run
first touchdown
first trophy
first time making the newspaper

First heart-felt conversation
first girlfriend
first anniversary
first breakup
first makeup

Nothing like the moment you start to see yourself as a man
first demand for privacy from your parents
first time making some of your own choices
first time having your head spin in social circles
nothing like the first

His Faith

Dedicated to Cecilio Germán

Up early with the sun, knees sore from prayer
then phone calls and home visits to neighbors
amidst his own pain:
dialysis three times a week
weakened body needing rest
shivers, colds, fevers, coughs, pain
paid their rents, funded their groceries
until they stood on their own two feet

He understood
when you arrived in the USA
ain't no boots, ain't no straps
burdens of others strapped on his back
he carried the cross

"Dwelling under the shadow of the Almighty
always believing and trusting in the Lord"
these were his words
on the tip of his tongue
an encouragement to others

My father pastored a herd of men
that were like fatherless children
along the righteous path
through tranquility, temptation and turbulence
reprimanded when necessary
never abandoned
rather reminded
me, you, them
"The Lord awaits you"

Su Fe

Dedicado a Cecilio Germán

Levantado temprano con el sol, rodillas adoloridas por orar
luego llamadas telefónicas y visitas a casas de los vecinos
en medio de su propio dolor:
diálisis tres veces por semana
cuerpo debilitado necesitando descansar
escalofríos, resfriados, fiebre, tos, dolor
pagó sus alquileres, financió sus compras
hasta que se pararon sobre sus propios pies

Él entendió
cuando uno llega a E.U.A.
no hay botas, no hay correas
cargas de otros atadas a su espalda
llevó la cruz

"Morando bajo la sombra del Omnipotente
siempre creyendo y confiando en el Señor"
estas fueron sus palabras
en la punta de su lengua
un estímulo para los demás

Mi padre pastoreó una manada de hombres
que eran como niños sin padre
por el camino correcto
a través de la tranquilidad, la tentación y la turbulencia
reprendió cuando fue necesario
nunca abandonados
más bien recordados
yo, tu, ellos
"El señor te espera"

Final Moments

My sisters and I held things together for as long as we could
my father was the strongest man we knew
the doctor came to the waiting room
"The time has come"
we cried as we walked into his room

We brushed his hair back
knelt by his side
his hand was cold in mine
outside his window the snow covered the ground

His favorite merengue played in the background
we waited for his final breath
we remembered his jovial dancing
his signature moves
we laughed together

Siblings huddled close
his breaths became shorter
squeezed out screams
emotions seesawed
down:
we didn't want him to suffer
this had to end
more short breaths
up:
was that his last breath?
we wanted him here
we wanted more moments
down:
landed in a new reality
his final moment came
we let him go

Momentos Finales

Mis hermanas y yo mantuvimos todo mientras pudimos
mi padre fue el hombre más fuerte que conocimos
el doctor vino a la sala de espera
"El tiempo ha llegado"
lloramos cuando entramos en su habitación

Cepillamos su pelo hacia atrás
arrodillados a su lado
su mano estaba fría en la mía
afuera de su ventana la nieve cubría el suelo

Su merengue favorito sonaba en el fondo
esperamos su último aliento
recordamos su baile jovial
sus movimientos característicos
nos reímos juntos

Hermanos acurrucados cerca
su respiración se hizo más corta
suprimidos los gritos
emociones sin balance
bajas:
no queríamos que sufriera
esto tenía que terminar
más respiración corta
altas:
¿Fue ese su último aliento?
lo queríamos aquí
queríamos más momentos
abajo:
aterrizó en una nueva realidad
llegó su momento final
lo dejamos ir

En Memoria Eterna

Cecilio German

Noviembre 30, 1947 - Febrero 13, 2022

El que habita al abrigo del Altísimo Morará bajo la sombra del Omnipotente. Diré yo a Dios: Esperanza mía, y castillo mío; Mi Dios, en quien confiaré. El te librará del lazo del cazador, De la peste destructora. Con sus plumas te cubrirá, Y debajo de sus alas estarás seguro; Escudo y adarga es su verdad. No temerás el terror nocturno, Ni saeta que vuele de día, Ni pestilencia que ande en oscuridad, Ni mortandad que en medio del día destruya. Caerán a tu lado mil, Y diez mil a tu diestra; Mas a ti no llegará. Ciertamente con tus ojos mirarás Y verás la recompensa de los impíos. Porque has puesto a Dios, que es mi esperanza, Al Altísimo por tu habitación, No te sobrevendrá mal, Ni plaga tocará tu morada.

Funeraria Díaz-Healy
Lawrence, Massachusetts

GLOSSARY

Caramel Translations:

mi dulce de leche	my sweet milk (fudge)

Café Con Leche Translations:

café con leche	coffee with milk
Azúcar	Sugar
Sabor	Flavor
bebiendo despacio	sipping slowly

Lengua Translations:

Mi batalla con el lenguaje	My battle with language
Complicado	Complicated
soy un poquito de todo	I'm a little bit of everything
pero completamente nada	but completely nothing
inglés	English
la tambora	the drum
inglés sin barreras	English without barriers
español - poema	Spanish - poem
femenino	feminine
un problema	a problem
Saboreando limóncillos	Savoring mamoncillos (Spanish Lime)
con-con	(Dominican slang for stick rice)
Sancocho - lengua	Beef stew - tongue
sazón	seasoning
mi estilo de hablar	my speaking style
a veces refleja la calle	sometimes it reflects the street

Black Denial Translations:

peinao	hairdo
derizao	perm
Oye primo	Listen, cousin
piel	skin
miel	honey
la tambora	the drum
colorismo	colorism
hora	hour
historia	history
Interesante a quien	Interesting who we
menospreciamos	undervalue
y a quien glorificamos	and whom we glorify
a quien, con nuestras	whom, with our
estatuas, honramos	our statues we honor
las aguas corren ondo	the waters run deep
indio trigueño moreno	indian, brunette, brown

Yo Soy Un Plátano Translations:

Yo soy un plátano	I am a plantain
verde y fuerte	Green and strong
mi gente	my people
seguro	for sure,
soy el maduro	I am the mature one
Cuatro por peso	four for a dollar

ACKNOWLEDGMENTS

All glory be to the Most High for the gift of writing and being able to voice myself. My parents, Melba and Cecilio: Your sacrifice has yielded many great things in my life. My wife, Lorena: This book is as much yours as it is mine. Your constant encouragement helped to make this possible. My children, Analíz, Zion and Sol: You are a gift from above that I do not take for granted. My sisters, Cristina and Shirley: Thanks for believing in me. My people in Lawrence, Austin and Tampa: Thank you for being in community with me. My editor, Tanya Manning-Yarde: Your thorough and honest feedback pushed me to go deeper. My book designer, Monica Ann Cohen: You helped bring BIT to life. My photographer, Jose Gabriel Estrella aka Fresh Creativo: You did amazing work on this project. My digital marketing strategist & web designer, Javier Roche: Your ongoing support helps Multicultural Classroom shine. My Spanish editor and translator, Jasmín García Ramírez. My brothers from the Soul Kaliber Movement (Jackson, Troy, Juni, Steve, Lamar, Cuba, Basil): You've been rocking with me and inspiring me since college. My brothers in the faith (Danny, Michael, Quincy, Denis, Ivan, Leonard, Shalaby, Andrew, Anthony): You've helped carry my cross when I've been too weak. My business coaches, Taína Benitez, Francesca Escoto, Waziri Garuba and Robert Kaplinsky: Your support has been invaluable.

Made in the USA
Monee, IL
29 May 2023

34915294R00052